Through My Eyes

Jessica Bertrand

Through My Eyes © 2022 Jessica Bertrand

All rights reserved.

No part of this publication may be reproduced, stored in a retrieval system, or transmitted, in any form or by any means, electronic, mechanical, photocopying, recording or otherwise, without the prior written permission of the presenters.

Jessica Bertrand asserts the moral right to be identified as author of this work.

Presentation by *BookLeaf Publishing*

Web: www.bookleafpub.com

E-mail: info@bookleafpub.com

ISBN: 978-93-95890-04-5

First edition 2022

Reflections

In the mirror we must look
Our flaws reflected, our beauty shook
Our eyes can't hide, the mirror knows
Our sins revealed, our stories told.

I Rise

Drowning
In your eyes
Falling
For love's disguise
Deeper
To the tides
Silently
From the dark, I rise

Transformation

Child
Innocent, Curious
Little one, Baby, Grown up, Elder
Experienced, Settling, Slowing
Wise, Cunning
Adult

Lawrence Bertrand

Laughter and fun you bring to life
Away on adventures, your dreams take flight
Worlds far beyond...........
Right here at home
Excitement you find wherever you roam
Near to my heart you will always be
Cherished and loved
Eternally.

Baby to Boy, you're growing so fast
Each day brings new memories to pass
Reach for the stars, believe in prayer
Treasure the small stuff
Remember to care
Always be kind, always be true
Never be someone else, always be you.
Dearest child of mine I want you to know
My love will be yours wherever you go.

Zachary Bertrand

Zachary, my second love
A gift you are, sent from above
Curious, you explore and find
Hidden joys, your face will shine.
Abound with your brother
Ruckus you cause
Your innocence will give me pause
    to stop and see just who you are.......
    the greatest parts of me by far.

Baby to Boy, you're growing so fast
Each day brings new memories to pass
Reach for the stars, believe in prayer
Treasure the small stuff
Remember to care
Always be kind, always be true
Never be someone else, always be you.
Dearest child of mine I want you to know
    My love will be yours wherever you go.

Wyatt Bertrand

Willful and Wonderful
You complete my life
Attention you command
Through your fearless acts
Tough little boy, I am truly blessed!

Baby to Boy, you're growing so fast
Each day brings new memories to pass
Reach for the stars, believe in prayer
Treasure the small stuff
Remember to care
Always be kind, always be true
Never be someone else, always be you.
Dearest child of mine I want you to know
    My love will be yours wherever you go.

A Lover's Journey

A simple smile to light your face
At the thought of that first sweet embrace
Still, you feel that moment now
Your eyes reflect what you can't show
What lies beneath, Love doesn't look
Unmasks your heart, your brain is shook
A silent prayer sent to above
A leap of faith, a trust in love
Weeks and years, like a symphony of stars
Mend, as one, our broken souls
This has been my Greatest sin
You, my love, my everything.

A Lover's Pleasure

Your lips on mine, I burn inside
Our hearts entwined, Emotions fly
Your sweet caress and tender touch
To chill my skin and make me lust.

As we are one, a perfect fit
Complete in body, mind, and spirit
Desire sparks, want fuels the need
The flames of love grow hot with speed.

The softest words brought to a whisper
The gentle throb of absolute pleasures
The endless calm, the candle light
In your arms I stay tonight.

A Fine Line

Love
Passion, Desire
Caressing, touching, feeling
Hearts, flowers, demons, dragons
Damaging, destroying, hurting
Malice, hostility
Hate

In Loving Memory

You've left this earth
You've gone to be
With others who've passed
Now memories.

Our hearts will cry
with tears in our eyes
As we fall silent
To say final goodbyes.

We'll celebrate your life
All the love that you shared
All the lives that you touched
All the people who cared.

Your purpose was fulfilled
So heaven called you home
To love and watch over from afar
An angel you've become.

Survive

Waves of emotion
Wash over me, sinking into
Darkness; I find light.

Dark Messages

12

Butterflies whisper
To heaven, on wings
Below to the wicked
My Angel brings.

Disturbed

Somber thoughts seeping
Into echoes of dreams
Tears falling
Somber thoughts seeping
Chaos reigning
Nothing as it seems
Somber thoughts seeping
Into echoes of dreams.

Dark Ages

Dark ages
Demons rising
Seeking souls
To feed the fires
Condemning all
No discrimination
All sins fall
To Hell's damnation.

Words

"A picture's worth a thousand words"
That is what they say
I prefer the written verse
To conjure as I may
Behind my eyes
The ink transforms
Words bleed onto pages
Helplessly, without fail
Masterpiece created.

Past The Stars

16

What is above
Beyond our reach
The product of
What is above
How shall we prove
How can we teach
What is above
Beyond our reach

A Tear

The smallest drop
Holds it all
Every emotion
Every thought
Until it falls

Wandering Thoughts

The hour grows long
My heart beats heavy
Every second an eternity

A prisoner I am
To wandering thoughts
The hour grows long

Keeping time
The rhythm flows
My heart beats heavy

The clock plays its song
Tic-toc, tic-toc, tic-toc
Every second an eternity

Blaze

Flames, all consuming
Embers glowing
Ashes behind
Memories.
Behind ashes
Glowing embers
Consuming all, flames.

Night Terrors

Answer this
Before you go
Can you tell me
Do you know
Either way
From now till then
Gather thoughts
Harness sins
Implore the night as
Jasmine wakes
Kneel beneath the
Lightless sky
Memories flash through your mind
Never keeping sync with time
Open hearts
Prepare to see
Question life,
Reality
Silent whispers
Truths
Unveiled
Vision blurred
With salty tears
eXtreme emotions
Yell their release,
Zero noise from with in

Wild Secrets

A hall of darkness
Beyond........unknown
Calls beckon
Desire follows
Echoes dance
Forming songs
Gradually you
Hear their voice
Intelligence amidst the noise
Just a glimpse
Keep moving on
Listen for that
Moment when
Neither sounds
Or songs
Peirce the deep
Quest to
Reveal
Secret
Truths
Uttered silently
Veiled
With in
eXactly personal
Your greatest sins
Zap your soul

www.ingramcontent.com/pod-product-compliance
Lightning Source LLC
Chambersburg PA
CBHW061326140726
47998CB00007B/2574